T0142515

IN THE BEGINNING

A Simple Story of Creation

MANDY HAYNES

WestBow Press books may be ordered through booksellers or by contacting:

WestBow Press
A Division of Thomas Nelson & Zondervan
1663 Liberty Drive
Bloomington, IN 47403
www.westbowpress.com
844-714-3454

ISBN: 979-8-3850-0658-8 (sc)
ISBN: 979-8-3850-0660-1 (hc)
ISBN: 979-8-3850-0659-5 (e)

Library of Congress Control Number: 2023916723

Print information available on the last page.

WestBow Press rev. date: 10/04/2023

WESTBOW
P R E S S®
A DIVISION OF THOMAS NELSON
& ZONDERVAN

IN THE BEGINNING

A Simple Story of Creation

In the beginning
there was
GOD.

GOD
created
the earth.

Then GOD Created

a beautiful garden.

In this
Garden,

HE put
all the animals.

GOD
needed someone
to take care of
the garden

So HE
Created
man and woman.

GOD named them
Adam and Eve.

They were the
first people.

GOD
loved
them.

And
GOD
loves you!

Paste Photo of
your child here

Printed in the United States
by Baker & Taylor Publisher Services